Contents

Maps and Illustrations

Map Guide to American

Migration Routes,

1735-1815

Map Guide to American

Migration Routes,

1735-1815

William Dollarhide

Heritage Quest, a division of AGLL, Inc.
Bountiful, Utah
1997

HER.Rm.
973
DOL

United States. Territorial Expansion,
United States -- Historical geography.
Migration routes -- United States.

Copyright © 1997 by William Dollarhide and AGLL, Inc.
All Rights Reserved

Published by Heritage Quest, a division of AGLL, Inc., Bountiful, Utah

Printed in the United States of America

2001 2000 1999 1998 1997   5 4 3 2

No part of this book may be reproduced or utilized in any form or by any means,
electronic or mechanical, including photocopying, recording, or by any information
storage and retrieval system, without permission in writing from the author and/or
publisher in any manner whatsoever except in the case of brief quotations
embodied in critical articles or reviews.

ISBN 1-877677-74-4

Preface

This book identifies the important overland migration routes used by Americans from about 1735 to 1815, a period during which the French-Indian War, the Revolutionary War, and the War of 1812 all played a critical part in the development of improved roads in America. The wagon roads identified begin with the King's Highway of 1735 from Boston to Charleston and end with the roads resulting from the War of 1812 in the Old Southwest.

All of the illustrated routes precede and exclude any steamboat routes, canals, or railroads. The intent of this *Map Guide* is to show the routes over which migrating families could travel overland in America before the industrial revolution. The first commercial steamboats began operating on American rivers as early as 1812, but did not begin to dominate river transportation until after 1816, when the first flat-bottom riverboat was built. The first canal of significance was the Erie Canal of New York, completed in 1825. The first commercially viable railroads did not appear in America until the early 1830s.

A description of "wagon roads" as migration routes may need clarification. In colonial America, people could travel anywhere by foot or horseback. But to pack your family and belongings in a horse-drawn conestoga wagon and travel perhaps hundreds of miles, an "improved" roadway was necessary. The road had to have at least a clearing through the trees and bridges or ferries for crossing streams.

The historical events that led to the opening of the Old Northwest and Southwest for settlement are discussed to demonstrate the importance of the time periods and historical factors that preceded the migrations of Americans. These events are important to understand why and when certain wagon roads became available for the first time.

The routes illustrated are the roads a family historian needs to identify in order to learn how his or her ancestors moved from one place to another. The maps can be used as a method of understanding the places where an ancestor may have passed (or stopped to see a daughter married off, have babies, or build a cabin for the winter) en route to their final destination.

In addition to the various histories of travel in America, American history atlases, historical maps, and other resources used to compile this work, one other important reference was needed: a *Rand - McNally Road Atlas* TM since most of the migration routes of our ancestors are still being used to this day. A current road atlas can be used to see details not shown in this *Map Guide.* Nearly every historic migration trail can be located on a modern map. Today they are known as Interstate, U.S., or State Highways.

Of course, the old Indian paths and river valley roads may not be exactly the same today. The old roads have been straightened, flattened, bridged, tunneled, and paved into superhighways. But the historic routes crossed the same mountains, passed through the same valleys, and forded the same rivers as today. Therefore, a modern designation is described for each historic wagon road, i.e., a state route, a U.S. highway, or an Interstate highway.

An earlier version of the text and maps in this book appeared in a series of three articles by the author in the *Genealogy Bulletin* (issues 22, 23, and 28), a magazine published by AGLL of Bountiful, Utah. The text has been revised for clarity and continuity within this context, and all of the maps were drawn anew by the author specifically for this publication.

Colonial Roads to 1750

The First American Highway

Beginning with the first settlements of the early seventeenth century, all American colonies were limited to the Atlantic seacoast and short distances up a few navigable rivers. For over 100 years, there were few excursions beyond the safety of these eastern harbors. With the threat of hostile Indians, impassable mountains, and little need for more living space, there were few colonists willing to migrate westward.

The roads over which a wagon could travel were limited to the coastal regions or up a few river valleys, such as the Connecticut, Hudson, or James River valleys. The possibility of traveling into the wilderness except on foot or horseback was not desireable or advisable, particularly by Puritan churchmen who equated the dark forests with the darkness of evil. Therefore, the first American highway was a coastal route that connected the original colonies north and south and never strayed far away from sight of the Atlantic Ocean.

The Boston Post Road and The King's Highway

By 1664, after England had "liberated" Manhattan Island and the Hudson River settlements from the Dutch, King Charles II informed his governors in New York and New England that he would be pleased if there were a communication established between his colonies. Subsequently, a crude riding trail was created for mail service between Boston and New York which became known as the Boston Post Road. The trail followed the same route as what is today the Massachusetts Turnpike from Boston to Springfield, and then down the Connecticut River, and finally to New York City. Later another post road connected Boston to Providence, Rhode Island, then down to the Connecticut coast.

However, it was decades before these trails were sufficiently improved to allow for wagon traffic or stage coaches to carry passengers. According to a journal written in 1704 by an intrepid woman who (on horseback) had accompanied a postman along this road... "unless someone followed a mail carrier, few travelers would be able to *find* the Boston Post Road."

Sailing ships remained the primary mode of transportation between the colonies well into the 1750s in America. Local overland roads that did exist were branches out from the major seaport cities, such as Boston, Philadelphia, or Charleston, and these were rarely more than twenty to thirty miles in length.

In keeping with the King's wishes, it was the old post routes that were to eventually become the "King's Highway". By 1750, a continuous road existed for stagecoach or wagon traffic from Boston, Massachusetts to Charleston, South Carolina, but only when the weather was cooperative.

By the time of the Revolutionary War, the King's Highway was a road from Maine to Georgia, providing a means of commerce between the colonies. But the significance of the King's Highway as a unifying factor between the colonies was only felt for some twenty-five years before the war. Of course, the colonies did unite. And it was in no small part due to the King's Highway linking them together. In fact, it would have been virtually impossible for the colonies to coordinate their war efforts against the British without the King's Highway. This road became the mustering point for several battles of the Revolutionary War including the final battle at Yorktown.

The King's Highway Today

■ **Boston to New York City.** Regular stagecoach travel could be accomplished between Boston and New York by the mid 1740s. Prior to that, the post routes were narrow trails that challenged riders on horseback, let alone a wagon. About the same time, alternate routes from Boston to New York developed. All of them can easily be found on a modern road atlas. For example, the Lower Route left Boston by way of Dedham and on south to Providence, Rhode Island. It connected Mystic, New London, New Haven, Fairfield, and Greenwich, Connecticut; then Rye, New York to Kingsbridge and into New York City.

Referring to the road as the the "King's Highway" came into disfavor during the Revolutionary War. The "Boston Post Road" is still the name used for many sections along this route today in Massachusetts, Connecticut, and New York, which was the main route of the early King's Highway. On a modern road atlas it is replaced in some sections by Interstate 95, but side roads parallel to the modern highway still exist with the old name.

■ **New York to Philadelphia.** A wagon leaving New York City for Philadelphia in 1750 had only a few ways to leave the island which are much the same as today,

except that bridges and tunnels have replaced most of the old ferries. You could cross the Hudson River to Newark, New Jersey. You could take a ferry from Manhattan to Staten Island, then cross the island to another ferry point at Elizabeth, New Jersey. Or you could leave Manhattan by a ferry around Staten Island to Perth Amboy, New Jersey. All of these crossings connected with the King's Highway.

From Newark, the King's Highway continued on the same general route as today's New Jersey Turnpike to Trenton. It ferried the Delaware River at that point, then followed the west side of the Delaware into Philadelphia. The route is fairly close to the modern Interstate 95.

■ **Philadelphia to Alexandria.** Although a wagon road was in place before 1750, travelers were more comfortable taking a boat from Philadelphia to New Castle, Delaware where the King's Highway was a portage link between the Delaware and Chesapeake Bays. (This was the site of a canal by the early 1800s). By 1745, that portage road was sufficiently improved to allow for regular stage-coach schedules. It was not an easy task, however, since the Susquehanna River had to be crossed some fifteen miles out of New Castle.

A German family en route from Pennsylvania to North Carolina in 1745 left a written record of that crossing. "On the side from which we approached there is a high sandy bank, and the wheels of the wagon sank to the axle in the sand, and were freed only after one and a half hours of work with levers and extra horses." It took two more hours to get their pair of wagons and three riding horses across the river by means of the ferry. They considered this quite lucky for "frequently travelers are detained here for an entire day".

The Philadelphia to Alexandria portion of the King's Highway was also called the "Great Coastal Road". It can be traced on

The King's Highway. As early as 1735, the coastal route of the King's Highway was mainly a postal trail between the colonies, and not a complete link for wagon traffic. By 1750, this wagon road linked all thirteen colonies, but was still not an easy road to follow. There were few bridges crossing rivers and streams, and during the spring, many parts of the road were impassable for weeks at a time.

a modern road atlas by following U.S. 40 (or I-95) from Philadelphia to Baltimore, then taking MD Hwy 2 via Glen Burnie to Annapolis. Now use the *Annapolis Road* (now MD Hwy 450) to Bladensburg, MD on the outskirts of present-day Washington, DC. The King's Highway crossed the Potomac River by ferry to Alexandria, Virginia, a seaport nearly as busy as Philadelphia or New York in 1750.

■ **Alexandria to Norfolk.** This section of the King's Highway (circa 1750) was often called the "Potomoc Trail". The first part of the road, from Alexandria to Fredericksburg, passes near some of the grand plantation mansions of Virginia, including George Washington's Mount Vernon.

But the leg from Fredericksburg to Williamsburg was abandoned long ago, including the road to Yorktown taken by the American troops during the Revolutionary War. That section of road was often flooded for weeks at a time, and even horseback riders had difficulty carrying mail along this route. Yet, it was the only access by wagon road to the colonial capital of Virginia from the West.

After inspecting the postal stations on this road, Benjamin Franklin made editorial complaints about the road in his newspaper, which may have contributed to its disfavor and, eventually, the disfavor of Williamsburg as Virginia's captial. (Ironically, it was precisely this disfavor that has preserved the beautiful old city of Williamsburg as an authentic relic of the colonial period).

After the Virginia capital was moved to Richmond in 1779, the King William-New Kent section of the King's Highway fell into disrepair. It was replaced by a route taken by what is now U.S. Hwy 1 (I-95) from Fredericksburg to Richmond, then U.S. Hwy 60 (I-64) from Richmond to Norfolk.

To follow the section of the pre-1779 King's Highway from Alexandria to Norfolk today, take U.S. 1 (or I-95) from Alexandria to Fredericksburg (Spotsylvania County),

Virginia, then U.S. Hwy 2 through Bowling Green (Caroline County) and then southeast on VA Hwy 721. Follow this or various other local roads until you cross the Mattaponi River into King William County. Then cross the Pamunkey River into New Kent County. The towns of King William and New Kent were both stopping points along the King's Highway en route to Virginia's colonial capital of Williamsburg, some 20 miles southeast of New Kent. From Williamsburg, a traveler could continue on a wagon journey to Yorktown, then on to Hampton, where a ferry crossing to Norfolk was possible.

■ **Norfolk to Charleston.** Leaving Norfolk, Virginia, a traveler on the King's Highway began a difficult trek through and around the lowland swamps of the tidewater areas of Virginia and the Carolinas. Many fords were necessary along this route, which followed present-day U.S. Hwy 58 from Norfolk to Suffolk, VA, then into North Carolina via what is now NC Hwy 32, skirting west to avoid the Dismal Swamp and then south to Edenton (Chowan County), North Carolina.

From the Quaker communities around Edenton, the old highway followed what is now U.S. Hwy 17 to New Bern, an important seaport and the early colonial capital of North Carolina. From New Bern, the highway bypassed White Oak and Angola Swamps in a fairly direct line to Wilmington, North Carolina at the Cape Fear River. As Hwy 17 does today, the old road continued on to Georgetown, SC and finally to Charleston, the colonial capital of South Carolina, and the southern terminus of the King's Highway prior to the Revolutionary War period.

From Boston, the distance to Charleston on the King's Highway was about 1,300 miles. It was possible to travel by wagon and, in most cases, average about 20-25 miles per day. Therefore, the entire distance would have taken at least two months.

The Lancaster Road

The Susquehanna River is a natural route to the interior of Pennsylvania. But the earliest western migrations out of Philadelphia had no access to the Susquehanna without first traveling to the mouth of the river in Maryland, a rather roundabout journey. The first overland road to the present-day city of Lancaster and then on to Harrisburg at the river began as early as 1725. The Appalachian valleys north and south of the Lancaster Road and rivers flowing into the Susquehanna River were the routes used for the earliest settlements in eastern Pennsylvania. For example, Lancaster County, Pennsylvania, formed in 1727, was first settled as a result of this road, which provided access to the Conestoga River Valley. The Lancaster Road is easy to locate on a modern road atlas — it is the same as the old Philadelphia Pike (U.S. 30 and PA 340) from Philadelphia to Lancaster, then the old Harrisburg Pike (PA 230), following a route about 10-15 miles south of the modern Pennsylvania Turnpike (I-76).

The Fall Line Road

The "fall line" is a geographic feature which acts as a separation line between the river tidelands and inland elevations on the Atlantic coast. Caused by erosion, it defines an east and west division between "upper" and "lower" elevations stretching from Maryland to Georgia.

By about 1735, the **Fall Line Road** cut off at Fredericksburg from the King's Highway, and continued to points south following the fall line, the first interior route into Virginia, the Carolinas, and as far south as the Georgia line.

If you want to know how an ancestor traveled from Pennsylvania or Maryland to the interior of the Carolinas before 1750, the King's Highway and the Fall Line Road were probably the routes they took. It is easily located on a modern road atlas as US Highway 1, passing through all of Virginia, North Carolina, South Carolina, and on to the settlement at Augusta, Georgia. A modern atlas will also show each of the counties they had to pass through. Check the formation dates on each county and you will learn when records for that county may be available for genealogical research, such as the early deeds, probates, wills, marriages, and so on.

The Great Valley Road

Before 1744, the "Great Warrior Path" was an Indian trading path from New York to the Carolinas. This trail marked the western frontier of the colonies, and no white man ventured across that line without fear of attacks from hostile Indians. In 1744, when a treaty with the Indians gave whites total control of the area east of the Great Warrier Path in Virginia, the way was clear for the path to evolve into the most heavily traveled road in colonial America. By the end of the 1740s, the **Great Valley Road** was the scene of large migrations into the wilderness of western Virginia, beginning at the Shenandoah Valley.

During the period 1745-1775, thousands of immigrants used this road. Many of them were Scotch-Irish families who had sailed from Ireland to Philadelphia or Alexandria. By the early 1740s, a connection from the Pennsylvania communities of Lancaster, York, and Gettysburg gave access to the Great Valley Road. This link was often called the "Philadelphia Wagon Road". By 1760, another northern access to this road was linked from the Pennsylvania communities of Shippensburg, Carlisle, and Harrisburg.

Migrations on the Great Valley Road resulted in many western settlements. It gave access to the first settlements on the Kanawha River such as present - day Charleston, West Virginia. By the early 1750s, the southwestern end of the road at

Big Lick, Virginia (now Roanoke) was extended and travelers could continue south into North Carolina or head southwest into eastern Tennessee. The earliest settlements in Tennessee were along the Clinch, Holston, and Powell River Valleys. All were accessed by way of the Great Valley Road.

The general route of the Great Valley Road today is called **U.S. Highway 11** (or I-81) and is very easy to locate on a modern map. Again, a genealogist can trace this route through the modern counties of Virginia today, find when these counties were created, and learn about records stored in the courthouses of these counties.

The Pioneer's Road

Before 1746, wagon trains from the Chesapeake enroute to the interior of Virginia were forced to head first to Philadelphia, most likely by boat. The reason for this out-of-the-way journey was the barrier of the Blue Ridge Mountains of Virginia. The first direct overland route through the mountains was from Alexandria to Winchester, the westernmost town in Virginia at that time. A road was completed in 1746 called the **Pioneer's Road.** The road followed closely to what is now U.S. Hwy 50.

The frontier town of Winchester became a northern access point of the Great Valley Road at Virginia's Shenendoah Valley. To get to this jumping off point, the Pioneer's Road negotiated the wilderness foothills west of Alexandria and passed through the crest of the Blue Ridge Mountains at Ashley Gap. With the Pioneer's Road as a more direct route west, Alexandria became a more popular port than Philadelphia for the many Scotch-Irish immigrants coming to America from 1746 up until the Revolutionary War.

The Upper Road

During the decade of the 1740s, the water transportation routes were no longer ade-quate to gain access to new farming areas. The upgrading of trading trails to full-fledged roads for wagon traffic was necessary. Another major route was needed to gain access to farm lands in the interior of Virginia and points further south. Filling this need was the **Upper Road,** which began at Fredericksburg (on the King's Highway) and continued across Virginia to North Carolina, but lying west of the Fall Line Road.

In the mid 1740s, the proprietary governor of the Granville District (approximately the northern third of North Carolina counties today), began issuing land grants to Quakers and others from the tidewater counties of North Carolina and Virginia. They were joined by Scotch-Irish immigrants who came in great numbers. The Upper Road, which began as a trail, was improved to become a major access route to these lands by about 1748. During the Revolutionary War, the Upper Road played a critical role in troop movements in the South, particularly the battles at Guilford Courthouse, King's Mountain, and Cowpens.

The Virginia portion of the Upper Road is one of the few wagon roads of our ancestors that cannot be easily traced on a modern road atlas. From the north, the route followed a path that is no longer a continuous road today, due to several man-made lakes along the way. From Fredericksburg, the general route of the Upper Road was west of present Interstate 85, and passed through and contributed to the settlement of the current Virginia counties of Spotsylvania, Louisa, Goochland, Powhatan, Amelia, Nottoway, Lunenburg, and Mecklenburg. The Upper Road at about the point of the North Carolina/Virginia line is nearly the same as Interstate 85, which continues southwesterly to Charlotte, North Carolina, and into Spartanburg and Greenville, South Carolina.

✦　✦　✦　✦

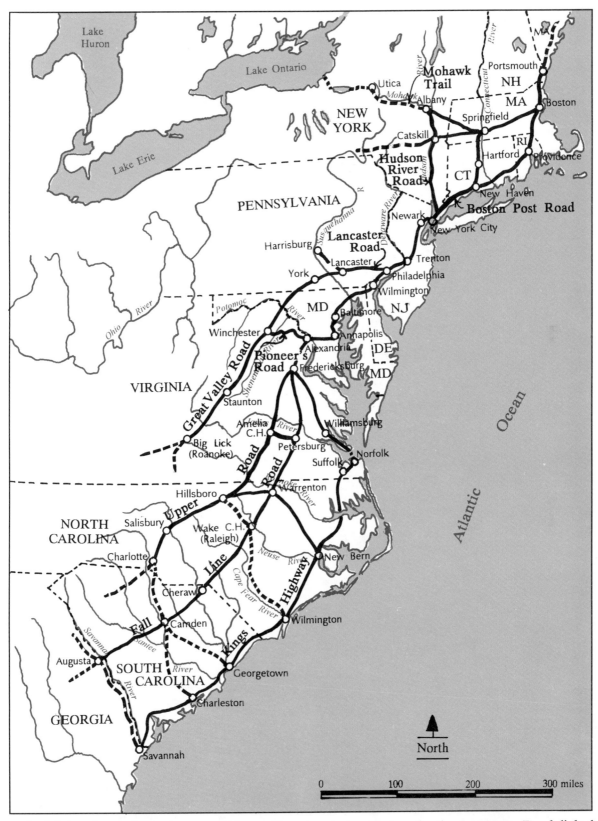

Colonial Roads to 1750. As one of the earliest east-west wagon roads, the **Lancaster Road** linked Philadelphia to Harrisburg before 1730. A connection from Lancaster to Winchester, Virginia, in the early 1740s created what was either called the **Philadelphia Wagon Road** or the **Great Valley Road.** The **Fall Line Road** crossed Virginia and the Carolinas and, eventually, into Georgia. By 1746, **the Pioneer's Road** had connected Alexandria to Winchester, Virginia, joining with the Great Valley Road. By 1748, the **Upper Road** became an important wagon route for migrations into the Carolinas.

Colonial Roads, 1750-1775

The Ohio Company and The French-Indian War

In 1746, a trading company was created by a group of investors in Virginia calling themselves The Ohio Company. The investors included Virginia's Governor, Robert Dinwiddie and Lawrence Washington (George Washington's half-brother), as well as several other prominent members of the Virginia gentry. The importance of this company in American history is that it was the driving force behind a series of events that not only led the British into a war with France, but the development of wagon roads into wilderness areas which were previously inaccessible.

The Ohio Company was interested in obtaining furs in trade with the Indians in the western regions of Virginia, which included Britain's claim of western lands never controlled by the British. But the Ohio Company's map of Virginia in 1746 was based on Virginia's Royal Charter of 1609. It described Sir Walter Raleigh's grandiose claim from "sea to sea" plus a northern boundary running generally from the Chesapeake Bay to Alaska, even though the areas west of the Appalachian Mountains were also claimed by both Massachusetts and Connecticut in their Royal Charters. It was mostly a moot point, however, since the area west of the Appalachian Mountains had been controlled by France since the days of LaSalle, some 150 years earlier. "New France", as it was called, consisted of an elaborate network of trading forts from Montreal to New Orleans.

Hoping to force the issue of ownership of these western lands, and with the encouragment of the Virginia colonial government, the Ohio Company financed numerous teams of traders. They traveled overland from Alexandria, Virginia, to the forks of the Ohio River (now Pittsburgh) then into the Ohio country where they met with great success in trading goods to the Indians in exchange for furs.

The "roads" of New France were the rivers and streams of the great Mississippi Valley. A series of connected trading posts were reached only by lightweight birchbark canoes. Some trappers covered as much as 100 miles in a single day, an incredible feat for the time. But, for all the time the French were in the region they never constructed a road longer than 13 miles in length and that was only to provide portage between rivers.

The Ohio Company paid more for the furs than the French, who had until then enjoyed a monopoly in trade with the Indians. In 1752, Indian tribes that had been previously friends with the French joined with the British and began raiding French trading posts. But the French were not to be overthrown so easily, and skirmishes led by the French in retaliation caused great losses to the Ohio Company's profits.

In 1753, the Ohio Company learned that the governor of New France, the Marquis Duquesne, was using Indians to erect a new series of forts, stretching from Presque Isle on Lake Erie, and including a new Fort Duquesne at the forks of the Ohio. Not pleased, the Virginia investors decided it was time to assert British authority in the area. British interests, i.e., Ohio Company interests, were being seriously threatened.

The political influence of the Ohio Company and the Virginia colonial government led to official British support of war with France. These were the factors leading to the French-Indian War of 1754-1763. This war forever changed the road map of the American Colonies, particularly the roads on which our ancestors traveled west.

Governor Dinwiddie and his fellow Ohio Company investors were very concerned about losing this rich trading area to the French. The Ohio Company hoped to encourage western expansion into these areas and create its own trading forts with the Indians. The British trading forts already in place on Lake Erie and Lake Ontario were having no difficulty in displacing the French, but the threat of this new Fort Duquesne was more than they could tolerate. It was located at the most critical and strategic crossroad for either French or British control of the territory north and west of the Ohio River. It came down to whoever controlled the forks of the Ohio would dominate the northwest.

Braddock's Road

In October 1753, a 21-year-old George Washington took the King's Highway from Williamsburg to Alexandria, Virginia. As the leader of a small group of experienced woodsmen, he was under orders from Governor Dinwiddie to find the best overland route to Fort Duquesne. Once there, he was to deliver a message to the French commander. "Get out of Virginia!" (actually... Pennsylvania, but geography was then a new science).

From Alexandria, George Washington traveled along the Potomac River to Fort Cumberland, a new fort still under construction. From there, his small band followed the pack team route called the "Venango Trail" which the Ohio Company traders had used for several years. But, in the course of his trip, Washington explored and recorded in his journal better ways to get to their destination, keeping in mind the possibility of a route suitable for a wagon road.

Washington was essentially an agent of the Ohio Company, who saw a wagon road as the one way of maintaining and supplying a British outpost and to support their proprietary interest in the forks of the Ohio River. The governor of Virginia had persuaded the British army to take possession of the area and to finance the mustering of troops and road construction. George Washington received a commission as Lt. Colonel and began recruiting colonials as soldiers to bolster the British forces against the French.

In early 1755, the British General, Edward Braddock, began supervising the construction of a wagon road through the wilderness areas of Maryland and Pennsylvania following routes laid out by George Washington. At the height of the road building effort, there were about 3,000 men engaged in its construction.

Braddock's Road was the first road to cross overland through the entire Appalachian Mountain range. For the first time it allowed horse-drawn wagons to travel a great distance to the west. Braddock insisted that the road be 12 feet wide, a monumental undertaking. The road was successfully completed. However, due to some poor military tactics, Braddock failed in his military mission. His troops were completely surprised and overrun by the Indians supported by the French, and Braddock's troops were dispersed. General Braddock was mortally wounded in the battle and was buried along his road at Fort Necessity near the present town of Farmington, PA.

Most of the length of Braddock's Road is the same or near to **U.S. Highway 40**, a route that can be found on a road atlas today. So, get out your trusty *Rand McNally Road Atlas* and you can easily confirm the names of towns, counties, rivers, and mountains through which passed old Braddock's Road. The route starts at Cumberland, Maryland, and ends at Pittsburgh, Pennsylvania.

Forbes' Road

After Braddock's failure, there were several successful battles with the French for control of the Great Lakes area. But it was still necessary to advance on Fort Duquesne. In 1758, the British forces were commanded by General John Forbes. He ignored the pleas of Colonel Washington to use Braddock's Road again, which by now was heavily defended by the Indian forces of the French. Forbes' plan was to send Colonel Washington with a smaller force up Braddock's Road to keep the French occupied. He would then build a new road further north and sweep down on the French by surprise.

With up to 4,000 troops building the road at Laurel Hill, Forbes' finally arrived at Fort Duquesne. There he discovered that the French had abondoned the fort. The all-important forks of the Ohio has remained in British-American control ever since.

The modern route of Forbes' Road is generally the same as the Pennsyvania Turnpike (I-76). The exact route of Forbes' Road of 1758 began at Harrisburg, Pennsylvania. The historic forts and camps built by Forbes' troops along the way are easy to locate on your road atlas. From Harrisburg (Dauphin County) take U.S. Hwy 11 across the Susquehanna River to Camp Hill, Carlisle Barracks, and Shippensburg and continue southwest on to Chambersburg. To ease the difficulty of crossing Tuscarora Mountain which the Turnpike simply tunnels through, go around it as Forbes did. At

Chambersburg, use U.S. Hwy 30 and head west to Fort Loudon. Keep going on U.S Hwy 30 to McConnellsburg, then take U.S. Hwy 522 north to Fort Littleton and the Pennsylvania Turnpike. Take the Turnpike west to pick up U.S. Hwy 30 again at Breezewood.

From there it is a short distance to the restored Fort Bedford and Bedford Village. The turnpike follows a more southerly route, while Forbes' Road continues on what is now U.S. Hwy 30, crosses Laurel Hill, the biggest challenge to the construction of Forbes' Road, and on to Fort Ligonier and Greensburg (Westmoreland County), and finally, to Fort Duquesne, which General Forbes renamed Fort Pitt after his commanding general.

George Washington served with both Braddock and Forbes during the building of these roads and saw first-hand how the Indians cleverly avoided direct confrontation with General Braddock's formal ranks of soldiers. He later used these same tactics against the British with great success. Another participant of wilderness road building on both Braddock's and Forbes' Roads was a young Pennsylvanian named Daniel Boone, who was about the same age as George Washington.

By 1763, after the British were successful in removing them, the French ceased being landowners in North America except for New Orleans and a couple of forts on the St. Lawrence River (until some forty years later when an upstart Napoleon stole Louisiana from Spain). The western boundary of the thirteen British colonies in 1763 was the same as agreed upon at the Treaty of Paris twenty years later, which formalized the boundary between the United States and Spanish Louisiana as the Mississippi River.

With two new roads from the King's Highway to the forks of the Ohio River, water transportation down the Ohio and Mississippi was linked. These roads were to be the vanguard of a 100-year land boom.

But everything was note rosy yet. Out of the French-Indian War came an unexpected development. As a way of rewarding the Indians whose help was necessary in fighting the French, the British **Proclamation Line of 1763** was established at the Appalachian Mountains and by law prohibited any British colonial from settling west of that line. The vast western region was dedicated as "Indian Hunting Grounds".

Colonial Americans, and particularly the politicians and investors of the Ohio Company were not happy with this decision. In fact, they felt the King had stabbed them in the back. Some of the leading men of Virginia and the rest of the colonies began to think about the unthinkable, independence from Britain. The idea that the King would try to prohibit colonists from migrating west became one of the list of complaints "against tyranny" that would lead to revolution.

The Wilderness Road

In 1774 an empire building venture of the Transylvania Company sent Daniel Boone and some 30 heavily armed woodsmen to mark out a road through the Cumberland Gap of Virginia into Fincastle County (now Kentucky). By 1775, after much hardship and several skirmishes with Indians, Boone's men had blazed the first trail through the Cumberland Mountains and into the lush valleys of Kentucky. Unlike the soil along the Great Valley Road, the Kentucky topsoil was rich and plentiful and Kentucky was thought to be a farmer's paradise.

The fame of these Kentucky valleys created an almost frantic rush of migrations into this new territory. The Wilderness Road provided the means for the first settlements at Boonesboro, Harrodsburg, and many other sites to follow, mainly on or near the Kentucky River.

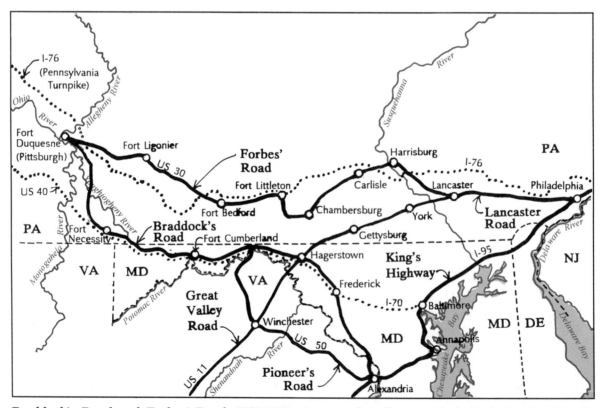

Braddock's Road and Forbes' Road, 1755-1758. As strategic military roads built during the French-Indian War, these roads advanced through the mountain areas of Maryland and Pennsylvania. They created western migration routes for wagon-loads of families.

In spite of numerous Indian raids on these early settlements, the lure of Kentucky persisted. The Wilderness Road became an extension of the Great Valley Road.

It did not matter that the first Wilderness Road was not really a road. It was a crude trail. Only pack teams could cross the mountains until 1796 when the trail was widened enough to allow a Conestoga wagon to pass. Many travelers before 1796 learned this fact only after traveling the length of the Great Valley Road and were then forced to abandon their Conestoga Wagons at Sapling Grove and pack their belongings on horses to undertake the ardurous trek into Kentucky.

Daniel Boone's contribution to American history was significant. At the time of the Treaty of Paris in 1783, Britain ceded to the United States the vast area from the Appalachian Mountains to the Mississippi River

mainly because the U.S. had thousands of settlers living in Kentucky by then. By 1792, when Kentucky became a state, over sixty thousand people had taken the Wilderness Road into Kentucky. They did it with great courage.

Because of the Wilderness Road, a Scotch-Irish immigrant family could start out from the end of their sea journey at Alexandria, Virginia, in 1796 and undertake a journey all the way to the middle of Kentucky in the same wagon. They had a sturdy Conestoga Wagon constructed of oak, with eight-inch-wide wheels, five feet high, and pulled by six draft horses. But all you will need for *your* journey is your Buick, a Visa card, and a *Rand McNally Road Atlas* to duplicate the route the immigrant train would have taken.

First, start moving west from Alexandria, Virginia, via U.S. Hwy 50 to Winchester (the same route as the Pioneer's Road). Next,

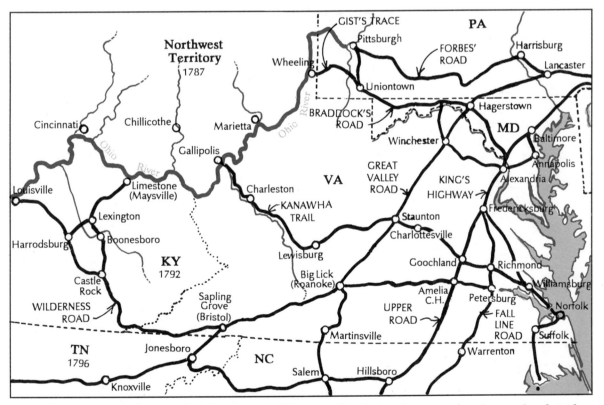

The Way West, 1775-1795. Daniel Boone's **Wilderness Road** was the route for thousands of settlers into Kentucky. Meanwhile, the western Pennsylvania routes provided an overland access to the Ohio River. After the Revolutionary War, western migrations on these routes continued to increase.

turn onto U.S Hwy 11 (or take Interstate 81 if you are in a hurry) and take that route the length of Virginia until you get to the Tennessee border (the route of the Great Valley Road). At the starting point of the Wilderness Road at Sapling Grove (now Bristol), take U.S. Highway 58 through the Cumberland Gap to Middlesboro, Kentucky. Then take U.S. Highway 25E to Mt. Vernon, Kentucky, then Interstate 75 towards Lexington. Leave the freeway at Exit No. 95, go about eight miles to the Kentucky River, and prepare to visit Fort Boonesboro State Park (the route of the Wilderness Road).

New York Migrations

The natural route of the Hudson River allowed for very early settlements north and northwest of New York City. Albany became the jumping off point for early excursions into the western or northern regions of New York, as well as points northeast into the upper areas of present-day Vermont. The convenient Mohawk River Valley became the primary route west. It was used first as a route for wagons to reach Lake Ontario, where boats could be used to ferry wagons and families to other Lake Ontario ports including Upper Canada (Ontario). This was the route of many Loyalists leaving the U.S. for British protection during and after the Revolutionary War.

From New York City to Albany, depending on which side of the Hudson River you travel, the route is now called U.S. Highway 9 or 9W, and the New York Thruway (I-87) follows the same north-south route. From Albany, the route is the east-west part of the New York Thruway (I-90). It is easy to locate on your road atlas.

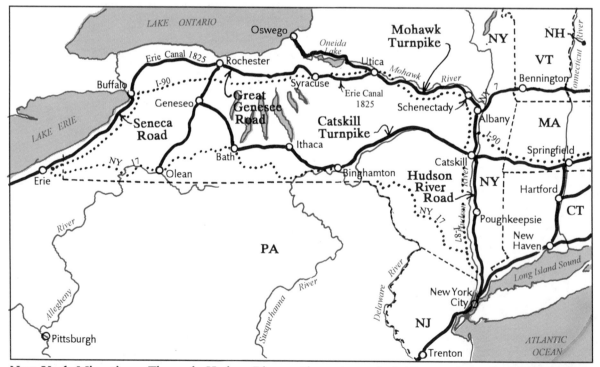

New York Migrations. The early Hudson River settlements reached Albany, where the Mohawk River Valley was a natural route to the west from Albany to Lake Erie. This route has gone from a horse path in the early 1700s, a wagon trail in the 1750s, the route of the Erie Canal by 1825, the New York Central Railroad by 1850, and the New York Thruway today.

Roads to the Ohio Country

After the French-Indian War of 1754-1763, France relinquished its claims to the great Mississippi and Ohio valleys. These areas now belonged solely to the British. The Mississippi River became the undisputed boundary between British and Spanish territory.

Britain surprised its American colonies with the Proclamation Line of 1763 which took away from the colonies the right to grant lands west of the Appalachian Mountains. In fact, the King's proclamation prohibited colonials from crossing the line at all. All land west of the Proclamation Line of 1763 was declared "Indian Hunting Grounds". However, the next decade was to lead to the American Revolution and the reversal of British policies in regards to western expansion and relations with the American Indians.

After the Revolutionary War and the creation of an American government, expansion into the western regions became a matter of national policy. The losers were the Indians who had supported the British during the war. For the next 100 years, the American policy towards the Indians became one of "Manifest Destiny", the self-proclaimed right of the United States to take possession of the continent by whatever means possible.

A Federal Land Grab?

The Manifest Destiny of the United States to expand from the Atlantic Ocean to the Pacific Ocean began at the very beginning of its existence as a nation. The Continental Congress of the United States began the process with the Ordinance of 1787, which was the original law providing for the creation of all new territories and states.

The national plan for expansion was part of ratifying the Constitution of the United States. The thirteen states were not only agreeing to the creation of a new Federal Government, they were giving up their claims to their western lands. Conflicting claims based on the Royal Charters of the original colonies were eliminated when the states of Virginia, Massachusetts, and Connecticut ceded their western lands to the U.S. Government. All three of these states had laid claim to the same area. By ceding their western claims, that issue was forever ended. In 1787 these lands became the Northwest Territory.

Soon after, Virginia gave up more land when its old Fincastle County became the state of Kentucky in 1792. Similarly, North Carolina ceded the area which became the Territory Southwest of the Ohio River in 1790, then the state of Tennessee in 1796. Georgia, with the most to lose, was a hold-out in ceding its western lands. Finally, in 1802, Georgia finally ceded its large western area, which was added to Mississippi Territory and which was to later became the states of Alabama and Mississippi.

Except for the states of Kentucky and Tennessee, all of these ceded western lands became the "public domain" with ownership in the hands of the Federal Government. Why were the thirteen states ready to give up these lands so easily? Was this an

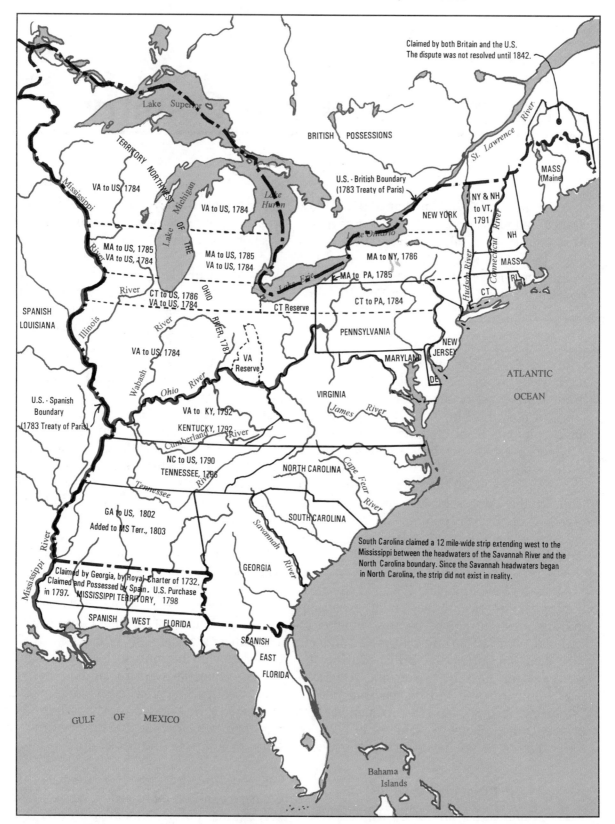

State Land Cessions, 1787-1802. By ratifying the constitution, the states ceded certain western lands to the Federal Government. North Carolina ceded the area that was to become Tennessee and Virginia ceded the area that became Kentucky. The Northwest Territory was created from land ceded by three states: Virginia, Massachusetts, and Connecticut. Georgia finally ceded its western lands in 1802, and that area later became the states of Alabama and Mississippi. Except for the states of Kentucky and Tennessee, these ceded lands became the "public domain" of the United States.

example of a Federal Land Grab? No, not really. Outside of a few customs fees and duties, the new Federal Government had no source of revenue. There were no federal taxes to run the government, no personal taxes, not even business taxes. For the first decade of its existence, the Federal Government was financed entirely by subsidies from the governments of each of the thirteen states.

The states gave up millions of acres of their western lands willingly for a very simple reason. As a landowner, the Federal Government would have a source of revenue by selling off land and the states could stop subsidizing this new federal monster they had created. As it turned out, land sales by the U.S. Government were to provide enough revenue to run the Federal Government for the next century without any other significant taxes levied on the American people.

The Land Business Begins

As an orderly plan for the creation of new territories and states was created, procedures for the sale of land by the Federal Government developed as well. Since the primary source of revenue to the new U.S. Government would be from the sale of land, migrations west of the Appalachian Mountains became a matter of national policy. Any new territories created were to have a Governor appointed. Provisions were made for a militia to maintain order and protect immigrants moving into the new lands. Congress determined that a territory could petition to become a state if there were at least 20,000 people living there.

As the first territory established in 1787, the **Territory Northwest of the Ohio River** became a proving ground for various methods of dividing up the land. It took another ten years before a consistent land measurement system was developed for the Federal

Government to begin selling land in the new territory. Meanwhile, as the feds developed their "cash cow" for making money selling land, some private land speculators got into the act.

Rufas Putnam's Great Idea

In 1785, a Boston businessman named Rufas Putnam had a great idea for making lots of money. As a former Revolutionary War General, he knew that the new United States was filled with thousands of former Revolutionary Soldiers, all of whom had been paid a suit of clothes and a promise of land "out west somewhere" in the form a certificate called a **Bounty-land Warrant**. These certificates had a set value of $1.25 per acre of land, but a soldier would have to travel to the great western wilderness and claim his parcel of land. The certificates could be legally "assigned", and the buyer of the certificate would then gain the claim to wilderness land "out west somewhere".

So Rufas devised a plan to buy certificates from former Revolutionary Soldiers, and for a fraction of their face value. He then figured out a way to combine these certificates for obtaining large tracts of land in the western wilderness. Rufas was to become a land speculator, using the time-honored rule of "buy low — sell high". First, he had to convince about ten of his business friends to invest money in his plan. A company was formed called the "New Ohio Company". By early 1787, the company was able to obtain warrants representing millions of acres of land "out west somewhere" purchased from the soldiers.

The New Ohio Company did not have trouble buying these certificates from the former soldiers. Everyone knew that going out west was dangerous. There were hostile Indians out there who had supported the British during the war and disliked Americans. There were no troops to protect settlers and there were no decent roads to get there. So when someone offered to buy your land warrant, you jumped at the chance to sell it. It is estimated that over ninety percent of all Revolutionary War Land Warrants were sold in this way.

The New Ohio Company agents set up shop in New York City. Their first "shop" was a soap box on a street corner where a hawker would call out to passers-by that he was buying Land Warrants. That soap box was on Wall Street. The practice of buying and selling Land Warrants is how the New York Stock Exchange got started.

Rufas Putnam's agents at the U.S. Capital in New York City were well connected. Rufas managed to convince legislators drawing up the Ordinance of 1787 to include a huge land grant for the New Ohio Company. Based on his assignments of bounty-land warrants, plus purchases on credit, his company's land grant was drawn on a map (north of the Ohio River, including all of present-day Washington County, Ohio), and exempted from the lands to be sold by the Federal Government. He also managed to gain much more land by agreeing to honor any soldier's Bounty-Land Warrants in the area granted to the company. All in all, Rufas and his associates managed to purchase seven million acres of land in the Northwest Territory for an average price of eight cents an acre. Some of the land grant was paid for using Bounty-Land Warrants and a small down payment was paid for the rest.

Rufas said he was willing to manage his company's large tract of land, sell to private buyers, and act as an agent for the Federal Government. Congress saw nothing wrong with this plan and voted for it, mainly because Congress had not yet developed a method to sell any land themselves. Essentially, the New Ohio Company became a land broker for the Federal Government and was selling land in the new Northwest Territory well before the Federal Govern-

ment began selling land there. Putnam told Congress he would pay for the land as soon as he sold it. What a deal!

The amazing part of this story is that Rufas Putnam pulled it off. He moved to the Ohio River and founded the town of Marietta, Ohio, where he began fulfilling his promise to Americans wanting to buy cheap farm land in the Ohio Country.

As a result, the earliest wagon roads into the Ohio Country were developed to get people to Rufas Putnam's land holdings.

The Gateway to the West

The first census of 1790 revealed that the U.S. had a population of 3,900,000 people. There was no enumeration for the Northwest Territory, but the entire white population was estimated to be about 4,300 people. Along with the settlements at Cincinnati and a few other Ohio River sites, there were already over a thousand families living near Rufas Putnam's Marietta land office on the Ohio River in 1790 — attesting to the success of Rufas Putnam's great idea.

Most of the earliest settlers came to the Ohio River settlements by way of **Forbes' Road** or **Braddock's Road,** both leading to Pittsburgh, which was becoming known as "the gateway to the west". Pittsburgh, in 1790, had nearly 400 houses, mostly brick, and was already an industrial center where sawmills provided finished lumber and where a small iron works was in operation. Pittsburgh had the basic necessities and the manufacturing capability for wagon wheels, barrels, horseshoes, and vitually any accessory a migrating family would need to continue a journey West.

Upon reaching Pittsburgh, the migrating families would buy or build their own flatboats for floating down the Ohio River to the new settlements. A flatboat was essentially a large rectangular wooden box, and was built to hold all of the family's possessions as well as livestock. A flatboat was built for a one-way trip down river. The boat itself would be disassembled at the end of the journey to provide some of the materials and nails needed for building a shelter.

The Boatmen

Commercial flatboats carried goods from Pittsburgh to the fledging settlements as well. Produce and grains were loaded at various river ports to be floated down to Natchez or New Orleans. These boats were often elaborate rafts with small cabins on them, including a stove for heat and cooking. But even the commercial flatboats were built to make a one-way trip down river, which might take two months from Pittsburgh to New Orleans.

The specialized occupation of a boatman was filled by rough-and-ready characters who saw every river port as an opportunity for drinking whiskey, boasting, and barefisted fighting. These men worked and lived on the flatboats during an era that lasted only about 30 years and is nearly forgotten in American history. They were mostly illiterate. There are few written records of their trips or exploits except by a few visting European travelers who recorded that they were generally unkempt, unsavory, and uncooth. But, in all reports, the boatmen were seen as absolutely essential to the navigation of boats down the Ohio and Mississippi Rivers. The boatmen had to be ready to fight off Indian attacks, as well as expertly navigate their boats through the obstacles of the river.

Migrating families might hire a boatman, recruited out of a local tavern in Pittsburgh or Wheeling. The boatman would help design and build the flatboat the family would use, and would be the navigator during the trip. Upon reaching the destination, the boatman would walk back up river to the nearest settlement and head for the nearest tavern.

Wheeling Rivals Pittsburgh

During parts of the year, the lower water levels and obstructions of the loop of the Ohio River from Pittsburgh to Wheeling made navigation difficult for the flatboats. Once Wheeling had been reached, it was

Ohio River Flatboat. From a drawing in 1796 in Victor Collot's *Voyage dans l'Amerique Septentrionale,* published in Paris, 1826. Reproduced from Archer B. Hulbert's, *The Paths of Inland Commerce: A Chronicle of Trail, Road, and Waterway,* "Chronicles of America" series, Vol. 21, New Haven: Yale University Press, 1920.

relatively free floating all the way to New Orleans.

In the early 1790s, a cut-off trail below Pittsburgh leading to Wheeling was developed. A family could leave Braddock's Road at Uniontown, Pennsylvania, then head northwest to Brownsville. After crossing the Monongahela River, the trail led to the present-day town of Washington, and finally to Wheeling. The cut-off road was called **Gist's Trace**. (Today this route is U.S. Highway 40).

At first, Gist's Trace was suitable for pack teams only, but was an important overland route to the Ohio River. But by 1796, the pack trail was improved to allow wagon traffic to pass. As a result of its location on the Ohio River and with this overland road access, Wheeling began to rival Pittsburgh as the "Gateway to the West". From Wheeling, the journey down the river to Marietta and Rufas Putnam's land office was only a three to four day boat ride on a flatboat.

Zane's Trace

One of the first land grants on the Ohio River went to a man named Ebenezer Zane, considered the founder of Wheeling, Virginia (now West Virginia). Zane had control of the land on both sides of the river and operated a ferry. With a virtual monopoly on ferry traffic at that point, he became a very prosperous man. Crossing the Ohio River from Wheeling gave access to an Indian trail into the interior of the Ohio Country. With Rufas Putnam's land holdings nearby and the creation of the new U.S. Military District, the Federal Government saw the need for upgrading the trail to provide access to these newly opened lands.

In 1796, Ebenezer Zane contracted with the Federal Government to construct the first wagon road into the Ohio Country. The road began at the Ohio River opposite Wheeling, then moved west on the same route today as U.S. Highway 40 (and Interstate 70) to the settlement at Zanesville, then southwest to Chillicothe, and south to the Ohio River again. A ferry ride across the Ohio River landed at Limestone, Kentucky (now Maysville), where a road connection from Lexington to the Ohio River was already well-traveled in the 1790s.

When **Zane's Trace** was first blazed, the dense forests of Ohio meant that road construction consisted of cutting the trees, leaving the stumps, and clearing out any underbrush to create a "trace" of a road. The passing wagons tended to form two rows of ruts, which were often the only visible evidence of a road surface. Grading or leveling improvements were made only at places where it was impossible to pass by wagon. On Zane's Trace, travelers referred to a "stumped" wagon as one that was highcentered on a stump or stuck between stumps — and the word is still used today when we are "stumped" over something.

Appeal of the Ohio Country

For twenty-five years after the Revolutionary War, the Ohio River was the primary destination of virtually all western migrations in the United States. This is where the first public land sales were opened, unlike the South, where Georgia did not cede its western lands until 1802. These new public lands were encompassed into a new Mississippi Territory. Extensive Indian control of western Georgia delayed settlements there. Migrations from the Atlantic regions into the southwest did not happen until well after the Northwest Territory had opened for settlement. For example, most land sales in Mississippi Territory did not begin until after 1800. Before that, the only real settlements in the South were located near the gulf seaports and the Mississippi River towns.

As the first area opened for settlement, the appeal of the Ohio Country was for fresh farm land. The Ohio River was the

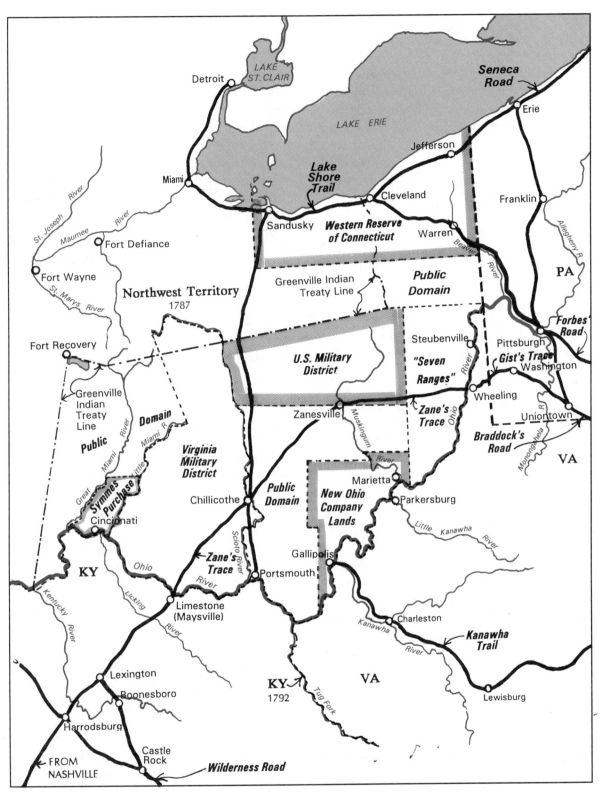

The Ohio Country, 1787-1800. Before 1790, land sales were limited to areas granted to private land developers, the two largest being Rufas Putnam's New Ohio Company and the Symmes Purchase. The Virginia Military District was set aside for military bounty-land claims, as was the U.S. Military District. The Western Reserve was settled mainly by people obtaining land grants from the State of Connecticut. The reserves were not part of the "Public Domain". The first Public Domain area opened in 1797 for sales to anyone was the tract of land called the "Seven Ranges". By 1800, there were Government Land Offices located at Cincinnati, Steubenville, Marietta, and Chillicothe and public land was being sold in all areas south of the Greenville Indian Treaty Line.

main highway leading to settlements on the principal tributaries, such as the Muskingum, Scioto, Miami, or Wabash Rivers. By floating downsteam on a flatboat, the Ohio River provided access to fresh lands to be cleared for crop farming, and where corn would grow so fast you could almost watch it rise. In addition, the soils between the Great Lakes and the Ohio River were well suited for wheat and other grains besides corn.

Except for some open areas within the interior parts of the Northwest Territory, the river areas were densely covered with huge trees, some over a hundred feet in height. Due to the wide branches and closeness of the trees, little sunlight penetrated to the ground below. Visibility was limited to a couple hundred feet in any direction, and there was an aura of darkness everywhere. However, with sparse underbrush below the towering trees, the trails were not nearly as difficult to follow as one would imagine.

The improvement of older roads was to have an impact on migrations to the Ohio Country. For example, travel on the **Great Valley Road** through the interior of Virginia continued the migration pattern established before the Revolutionary War. As an extension of the Great Valley Road, at Sapling Grove, Virginia (now Bristol), a wagon could head west through the Cumberland Gap into Kentucky, or continue south to Knoxville, Tennessee.

Back in 1788, the **Nashville Road** had been built by the Militia, linking Knoxville to Nashville, a distance of some 180 miles west. (Tennessee was not a state yet, and still part of North Carolina). The Nashville Road quickly became the primary route for east - west traffic through the interior of Tennessee. Earlier travelers had used the Cumberland and Tennessee Rivers as their main highways. With this link from Virginia to Knoxville, then on to Nashville, an important circle was completed. Nashville was

the northern end of the **Natchez Trace,** an old Indian trail.

By 1796, a road leading from Nashville connected settlements further north, all the way to Lexington, Kentucky. From there, a wagon road to the Ohio River linked overland travelers to Zane's Trace. It became possible to take a wagon from Natchez to Philadelphia, a trip that had previously been almost exclusively the opposite direction and mostly with the help of rivers. The Natchez Trace was first used as a return route for boatmen who had floated down the Ohio and Mississippi Rivers on flatboats to the ports of Natchez or New Orleans. (New Orleans was controlled by the French until 1803 making Natchez the southernmost U.S. river-port).

The children of the first settlers of Kentucky and Tennessee became attracted to the lands of the Ohio River as well. Settled well before the Revolutionary War, the green valleys of Kentucky and Tennessee were very rewarding for farmers. For the first few years, a farmer could watch his corn stalks jump out of the ground in great abundance. But the soil began to lose its potency within seven or eight seasons. The crops would begin to decrease in size and consistency.

Crop rotation and contour plowing for soil retention were techniques not used yet. The application of fertilizer to the soil was only practiced by a few enlightened German farmers in Eastern Pennsylvania before 1790. Those with large tracts of land learned they had to constantly clear and plant new fields and leave older fields fallow for a number of years before the soil would be suitable for a good crop again.

Many farmers gave up on their depleting soil. It was easier for some of the next generation to relocate and find virgin land to start anew. A young man with only a small farm and a growing family to support believed he had everything to gain by moving to the Ohio Country. The opening of roads to the Ohio River from several different starting points was also an incentive. The lure of the Ohio River settlements was for cheap land, and, once the land was cleared, farming could be easy again. There were only a couple of "minor" problems. A few Indians resented the white invasion into their hunting grounds. And it was not necessarily easy traveling to the Ohio River from anywhere.

Enter the Turnpike

The wagon roads to the Ohio River from Georgia, the Carolinas, and Virginia all converged on the **Wilderness Road** through the Cumberland Gap into Kentucky, then up to the Ohio River. Using state money, the new state of Kentucky upgraded the road through the Cumberland Gap to twelve feet wide in 1796. Other states were taking a different interest in their roads as well, particularly those roads which were being used for inter-state travel. The concept of a state-owned "turnpike", came during this period, because the building and maintenance of a heavily traveled roadway was an expensive undertaking. To pay for the roads, the states decided that "user fees" were in order.

In the 1790s, the direct route across Pennsylvania via Forbes' Road saw many easterners moving west to Pittsburgh or Wheeling to reach the Ohio River. As the start of the main route to the west from Philadelphia, the **Lancaster Pike** was the name given to the first road built using some "high-tech" road - building techniques borrowed from England. The route was virtually the same as the old "Lancaster Road" dating back to the 1720s; but the Lancaster Pike was significant, not for the route, but for the quality of construction. Completed in 1796, the new roadway was financed under a right-of-way franchise granted by the State of Pennsylvania to a private company.

For a distance of some 70 miles, a three-foot-deep trench was dug. This was filled with several layers of progressively smaller sizes of crushed rock, each layer tamped and packed solid. The workers crushed the rocks on the site, using only sledge hammers. The inventor of this road grading process was a Scotsman named Macadam. The result was called a "macadamized road". The process was first used in England in the early 1790s. The Lancaster Pike was the first macadamized road in America.

The process is still being used today. A macadamized roadway has a final application of melted tar mixed with gravel to provide a paved surface that is still used on farm roads all over the United States. The final "hot oil" teatment gave the roadway a hard, smooth surface, once traffic had solidly packed the top layer of finely crushed rock with the tar. Water actually ran off of the roadway, which was an unheard-of event on any American road to that date.

The Lancaster Pike was a huge success and became a profitable enterprise for the operators. Comfortable wayside inns soon catered to travelers all along the Pike and regularly scheduled stagecoach service ran from Philadelphia to points west.

Of course, travelers resented having to pay tolls for passage across the roadway, which was collected "per head", including cows, sheep, horses, or humans. But the speed and comfort one could travel on the Lancaster Pike by stagecoach or wagon was amazing. The all-weather road surface was the showplace highway of America. Stagecoaches pulled by six draft horses could maintain a consistent speed of 10-12 miles per hour. This was a giant step forward in transportation, because the best travel time possible before the advent of a macadamized road was about 20 miles per day (which is walking speed).

To trace the line of the old Lancaster Pike today, start at Philadelphia on US Hwy 30 and then take PA Hwy 340 into Lancaster. Both of these roads are easily located on a modern road atlas.

Further north, the route of the old Genesee Trail was to become the **Mohawk Turnpike,** the most important road for migrations across the state of New York. Following the valley formed by the Mohawk River, this road was continually improved due to the heavy demand of western migrations. By 1796, tolls were collected at several points along the way from Albany to Utica and later all the way to Buffalo. This is the same path which in 1825 became the route of the famous Erie Canal, and by 1850, the route of the New York Central Railroad. Today it is the same general route as the New York Thruway (I-90).

Below the route of the Genesee Trail, the Finger Lakes of western New York became water-borne transportation links. South of the Finger Lakes was another east-west road called the **Catskill Turnpike,** eventually linking the Hudson River to the Allegheny River.

A real-life journey to the Ohio River by a New York family might illustrate the difficulties of travel in those days. The family of Lot and Chloe (Ross) Hull was living near one of the Finger Lakes, Lake Canandaigua, New York, in the early 1800s. The Hull family decided to migrate to the Ohio Country where the land was fair and cheap, and the corn was said to grow to unbelievable heights. The route they traveled was outlined years later in a history of Pike County, Illinois, where children of the family later settled.

From Canandaigua, the Hull family made their way west to the frontier town of Geneseo and then south to the Allegheny River near the present-day city of Olean, New York. Here they built a flat boat on which they loaded all of their household

goods and provisions. A son tells the story: "They floated towards Pittsburgh, but enroute hit a snag in the river that capsized the boat. They saved only a few of their possessions, which they afterwards sold to the Indians for two canoes. They had enough clothing to last them for two years and provisions enough for one year, but when the boat was sunk all was lost. After securing the canoes they lashed these together and floated down the river to Pittsburgh. There Mr. Hull secured lumber and built a cabin on the canoes, after which he proceeded with his family in that manner to Marietta, Ohio. He there sold the boats, which netted him seven dollars and a half. He had a family of six children for whom to provide and, as indicated, was almost penniless when he located in Washington County, Ohio. By trade he was a carpenter, but he had lost his tools when his boat was sunk in the Allegheny River. The people of that locality, however, gave him work to do and he was able to buy tools on credit. After working for some time he was able to make an investment in land and purchased a hundred and fifty acres, building a barn to pay for this property."

Federal Land Offices

After the experiment with Rufas Putnam and a few other land developers, some not nearly as successful as Putnam, Congress determined that the Federal Government should establish its own land offices and sell the land directly to the public and forget about using middle men.

The first Government Land Office (GLO) in the Public Domain did not open for business until 1800, but thousands had already migrated into the Northwest Territory before then. The earliest settlers bought their lands from land developers like Rufas Putnam at his land office in Marietta, or they settled in the military reserves that had been set aside. For example, the Virginia Military District was an area set aside for bounty land warrants from Virginia soldiers of the Revolution (or their assignees). Since Virginia had reserved these lands prior to the creation of the Northwest Territory, the United States honored that reserve. A United States Military District in the Northwest Territory was also reserved. Both of these military reserves were outside of the Public Domain; that is, land grants were restricted to those holding Military Bounty Land Warrants. Another large tract of land in the Northwest Territory was the Western Reserve of Connecticut, which was also exempted from the Public Domain. The areas outside of these reserves were to be opened for sale to the general public through Government Land Offices established by the Federal Government.

Identifying the location of Government Land Offices is a good way to visualize the American population moving west. Once established, the GLO system was never changed, and dozens of offices were opened over the next 100 years. A land office was established after treaties with the Indians were complete and the region had been surveyed, at which time land sales could begin.

The physical location of a new land office was as close as possible to the land being sold, and on the leading edge of the western frontier. Locating the land offices is also a good way to understand when the development of roads first took place. For example, in 1800 the first four federal land offices were established in the Northwest Territory. They were at Chillicothe, Cincinnati, Marietta, and Steubenville, these being the only places land could be purchased in the Public Domain at that time. The first wagon roads did not extend far beyond the location of these land offices.

Ohio was the first state created from the Northwest Territory in 1803. As migrations into the Northwest Territory increased, and following plans set down in the Ordinance of 1787, Congress redivided the Northwest Territory, creating Indiana Territory in 1800, Michigan Territory in 1805, and Illinois Territory in 1809.

By 1810, there were a total of eleven land offices in the Public Domain; Canton, Chillicothe, Cincinnati, Marietta, Steubenville, and Zanesville in Ohio; Jefferson and Vincennes in Indiana Territory; and Huntsville, St. Stephens, and Washington in Mississippi Territory. Connect the dots between these towns on a map, and you will be defining the western frontier of the United States for 1810.

The National Road

In the enabling act of 1803, Congress decided to set aside five percent of the receipts from land sales in public domain areas of the new state of Ohio for the purpose of constructing roads. Enough money was collected by 1806 to begin planning for the **National Road,** the first interstate highway financed by the Federal Government. Some surveying and clearing of the right of way began as early as 1808, but the War of 1812 delayed the construction, and the work was not fully underway until 1815.

The entire length of the National Road today is easy to find on your Road Atlas. It was nearly the same as the present-day U.S. Highway 40 from Baltimore to St. Louis. The section from Baltimore to Wheeling was also called the "Cumberland Road", following closely to the earlier Braddock's Road. The enthusiastic legislators called for a roadway clearing sixty-four feet wide, a grand thoroughfare that would run from Baltimore to St. Louis. The road was to be a modern macadamized surface from end to end following the methods previously used so successfully on the Lancaster Pike. Good down'-'to'-'earth engineers prevailed, however, and a more conservative project ensued, with thirty-foot widths on flat open stretches, and down to one lane passages through mountainous areas. The final "hot oil" treatment of a true macadamized surface was never completed on the National Road. So basically, it ended up as a gravel road.

Had the engineers built the road the way Congress specified it, it would have rivaled any superhighway of today. One early decision in the building of the road, however, proved to be a wise one. All the bridges were built of stone rather than wood, and many of the bridges are still in use today.

When the National Road was completed from Baltimore, Maryland, to Wheeling, Virginia, in 1818, it became America's most heavily traveled road. But, as it turned out,

the construction methods were not perfect. The trench dug to hold the gravel in place ended up collecting water instead of draining it. As a result, the trapped water froze in the winter, expanding and loosening the rock base. This created potholes "the size of Rhode Island" as one traveler reported. The gravel surfaces of the Maryland sections were already in a terrible state of disrepair by the time the later Pennsylvania and Virginia sections were completed. But over the next twenty years, the road was completely reconstructed on its entire length. The engineering problems and squabbles with Congress were endless. The states, the Federal Government, and the private contractors building the road eventually settled on a way of building roads that has continued to this very day. It was the National Road where these lessons were learned the hard way.

For example, the states of Maryland, Pennsylvania, Virginia and Congress got into a heated debate about who was respon-

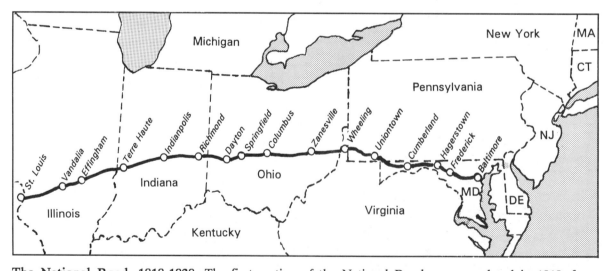

The National Road, 1818-1838. The first section of the National Road was completed in 1818, from Baltimore to Wheeling. This route was also called the "Cumberland Road" and was soon the most heavily traveled highway in America. The grading and surfacing made it by far the most comfortable road to travel for its day. Stagecoaches and commercial wagon traffic was heavy, with teams of wagons carrying grain and produce from the interior to markets in the East, and manufactured products to the West. Many taverns and inns catered to travelers, where the latest news and politics were exchanged around the roaring fireplaces. The road was completed across Ohio by 1828, across Indiana by 1832, and completed to St. Louis in 1838. In the 1840s, the road was continued to Jefferson City, Missouri. The towns along the National Road grew rapidly and became some of the most important trading centers in America. Baltimore benefited the most as the eastern terminal of the National Road, rivaling New York, Philadelphia, and Boston as the prime seaport of the United States. The same general route of the old National Road is very close to U.S. Highway 40 and Interstate 70.

sible for maintaining the road, Congress believing that the legislation authorizing the construction of the road said nothing about repairs later. The states felt that since they didn't own the road they shouldn't have to fix it. And, if toll gates were to be installed, who collected the tolls for maintaining the turnpike? The issue was not settled for several years, but eventually, the Supreme Court ruled that the U.S. Government could certainly finance the construction of roads, but that the finished roads should then belong to the states through which they passed, and that the states could then charge tolls for maintaining the highway. This is pretty much the same relationship that exists today between the States and the Federal Government as pertaining to Interstate and U.S. Highways in America.

Enter Steamboats, then Canals

In 1808, Robert Fulton demonstrated to the world that his steamboat could travel up the Hudson River from New York to Albany, against the current of the river, yet maintain a speed of five miles an hour. Fulton was not the first to use a steam engine to power a boat, but his *Cleremont* was the first steamboat to show the economic benefits of such a craft. Within another ten years, steamboats were to appear on virtually every navigable river in America.

The flatboat era ended with the introduction of steam-powered boats on the Ohio and Mississippi. But the real "riverboat" did not appear until 1816, when the first steamboat was built that placed the steam engine above the water line and added a second deck. Before that, Fulton's steamboat and later boats built on the Ohio River by 1812 were built like ocean-going vessels, which had too much draft to negotiate the often low water depths encountered on the rivers. By 1820, the familiar flat-bottomed riverboats powered by steam became the predominate mode of transportation on the Ohio and Mississippi Rivers.

Travel to the Ohio Country was to change significantly after the development of canals through New York and Pennsylvania. The Erie Canal was completed in 1825, and Lake Erie settlements in Ohio and Michigan boomed as a result. Only eight years later a family could travel from Philadelphia to Pittsburgh without ever leaving a canal boat. A canal from Philadelphia to Reading then west to Pittsburgh was completed in 1833. The stretch from Hollidaysburg to Johnstown was an exciting ride where the canal boats were towed over 2,000 feet in elevation up a series of inclined water raceways. By 1830 there were canals in the interior of Ohio and Indiana. And by 1850, railroads had made the old wagon roads to Ohio nearly obsolete.

Those who went to the Ohio Country before the riverboats or canals during the opening of the Northwest Territory negotiated rugged trails and suffered great hardships to reach a river where they had to build their own flatboats and find their new homes. That era lasted only about thirty years.

✦ ✦ ✦ ✦

Roads to the Old Southwest

Many of the first wagon roads our ancestors traveled were created for military purposes. For example, the first roads across the Appalachian Mountains, Braddock's Road and Forbes' Road, resulted from the French-Indian War of 1754-1763. These military roads opened the way for the great western migrations before and after the Revolutionary War and saw thousands of Americans moving into wilderness areas west of the Appalachian Mountains.

Before the Revolution, Daniel Boone blazed a trail through the Cumberland Gap and the route from Virginia to the interior of Kentucky was used by over 60,000 people by 1792. After the Revolution, the destination of most migrations was to the Ohio Country. Beginning as early as 1787, great numbers of Americans moved into the area northwest of the Ohio River. At the same time, the improvement of Kentucky and Tennessee roads by 1796 gave access to the interior of those new states.

Lagging behind these migrations was the development of the Old Southwest, the area of Georgia before it ceded its western lands to the United States Government. Georgia was a hold-out in ratifing the new Constitution of the United States because it would have to give up over half of its territory to the Federal Government.

In 1802, Georgia ceded its western lands. These Public Domain areas were to later become the states of Alabama and Mississippi. Soon after Georgia's land cession, America doubled in size with the Louisiana Purchase, an area that was loosely defined as the river drainage of the Mississippi and Missouri Rivers. But this vast area was not to become the scene of significant migrations until after the war of 1812.

Late Development in the Old Southwest

Unlike the large influx of western migrations to the north, the western migrations to the Old Southwest were late in developing for at least three reasons:

1. While the northern states were heavily populated and the demand for fresh lands was an incentive for migrations to the West, Georgia was sparsely populated. Georgia was the last of the thirteen British colonies settled in America (founded as a Royal Colony in 1732, some 112 years later than Massachusetts, for example). Most of Georgia's population in 1790 was within 25 miles of the South Carolina border.

2. Western Georgia was controlled by several Indian tribes, particularly the Creeks and Cherokees, for which the Federal Government had created "Indian Nations" by treaty, giving these tribes a great amount of political autonomy. Migrations to the west in Georgia were limited to areas not under control by the Indians.

3. The settlements of the Old Southwest were primarily on the Gulf Coast, easily assessible by sea. Political control of New Orleans was not transfered to the United States until 1803. Other early French/Spanish settlements, such as Mobile or Pensacola were mainly seaports with some river

traffic to the interior. American control of these areas was still contested by the U.S., France and Spain until well after 1800. It was the Louisiana Purchase in 1803 that forced political jurisdictions to be resolved by treaty after decades of cross claims. Thus, the development of areas that were to later become the states of Florida, Alabama, Mississippi, and Louisiana were some twenty years behind the states created from the Old Northwest, such as Ohio, Indiana, Illinois, and Michigan.

For these reasons, no compelling need existed for wagon routes to the Old Southwest until the first decade of the 19th century, some thirty years after the western migrations in the northwestern part of the United States had already begun.

The Natchez Trace

The only overland route in the Old Southwest before 1806 was the **Natchez Trace,** an old Indian trail beginning at Natchez on the Mississippi River and from there, running northeast to Nashville.

Most river traffic from the Ohio River to New Orleans was down-stream on flatboats or floating rafts. After completing their two-month journey from Pittsburgh to New Orleans, the boatmen returned north on foot or horseback by way of the Natchez Trace. Remember, steamboats did not begin on the Ohio or Mississippi Rivers until after 1812, and not in any great numbers until about 1816. Before that, negotiating the Mississippi River upsteam was a laborious undertaking, using long poles to propel the rafts along the shallow sides of the river.

By 1796, the Natchez Trace from New Orleans to Nashville, Tennessee was extended to Lexington, Kentucky, connecting with an existing route to Limestone, Kentucky (now Maysville) on the Ohio River, and

then into the Northwest Territory via Zane's Trace to Wheeling, and finally, on to Philadelphia via Forbes' Road. This was the return route of the boatmen who had floated down the Ohio and Mississippi Rivers.

But other travelers could take the **Nashville Road** completed in 1788. It linked Nashville to Knoxville, Tennessee, and from there to the **Great Valley Road** through Virginia and connecting to Philadelphia.

Historical Events Leading to the Opening of the Old Southwest

The United States declared its independence in 1776, fought a war, and at the end of that war, signed a treaty with England, Spain, and France. The Treaty of Paris of 1783 is when the United States first became a legally recognized republic in the eyes of the rest of the world. However, the United States of 1783 had some areas not yet under its control or in dispute with other countries.

For example, as a result of the original Royal Charter of Georgia of 1732, the United States laid claim to Georgia's western lands to the Mississippi River. But an area of the Georgia Charter (from latitude 31 degrees to latitude 32 degrees, 28 minutes) was also claimed by Spain. The U.S. claimed the area, but Spain actually possessed it. This area was left out of the Treaty of Paris, and the two parties entered into negotiations over the ownership of the disputed area. The dispute ended when the U.S. purchased that portion of land in 1797.

Soon after, the U.S. Congress created within that area a new **Mississippi Territory,** a new addition to the Public Domain of the United States. The existing trading towns of New Orleans, Natchez, and Mobile became entry points to this new American

Territory, but American traders had been moving into these areas well before 1797. The United States had free use of the Mississippi River to float goods and produce to New Orleans under conditions of the 1783 Treaty of Paris.

In the first decade of the 1800s, Napoleon Bonaparte was waging war on Europe. In 1802, his victory over Spain gave him Louisiana as spoils of war, a vast area of North America that had been solely in the hands of the Spanish for centuries. Napoleon gave the Spanish a couple of small areas in northern Italy in exchange for Louisiana. In early 1803, being short of cash, Napoleon let the American ambassador in Paris know that he might be interested in selling Louisiana to the Americans.

In 1803 the United States purchased Louisiana from France, acquiring New Orleans. In November 1803, Robert Livingston and James Monroe represented the United States in Paris and concluded a treaty with France to take ownership of Louisiana (for about three cents per acre).

Immediately, the U.S. created two new territories in the Louisiana Purchase: Orleans Territory (which followed the modern bounds of the state of Louisana; and Louisiana Territory, later to be named Missouri Territory. Soon after, President Thomas Jefferson launched the famous Lewis and Clark expedition to explore the new Louisiana Territory. Again, the new territory was added to the Public Domain.

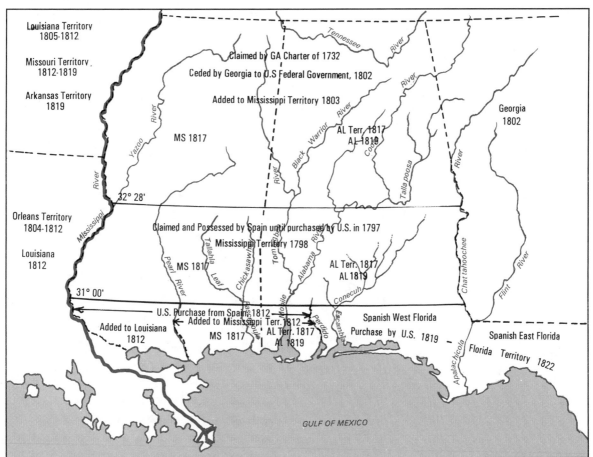

Principal Lines of the Old Southwest, 1797-1822. In 1797 the U.S. acquired from Spain the area between Latitudes 31 degrees, and 32 degrees, 28 minutes, stretching from the Chattahoochee River to the Mississippi River. In 1798 Congress made this area Mississippi Territory. When Georgia ceded its western lands in 1802, they were officially added to Mississippi Territory in 1803. A portion of West Florida was added to the State of Louisiana and Mississippi Territory in 1812, and the remainder of Florida was purchased from Spain in 1819.

Georgia finally ceded its western Lands to the United States Government in 1802. Georgia's ceded area was then officially added to Mississippi Territory by an 1803 act of congress, more than doubling its size. The enlarged Mississippi Territory was an area the size of the modern states of Alabama and Mississippi, less a portion of West Florida not yet in the hands of the U.S.

By acquiring Louisiana, the United States also thought it had obtained title to West Florida, but the Spanish differed with that opinion. This panhandle area of Florida did not become part of the United States until 1812, when the U.S. and Spain signed a treaty and the U.S. paid cash for the areas west of the Perdido River. As a result, Pensacola, Mobile, and Biloxi became part of the United States. To finish off the land acquistions in the area, in 1819 the United States purchased the Florida Pennisula from Spain, fixing the boundaries of the Old Southwest to the way they are today.

The United States was selling land to settlers in its Public Domain areas of the Territory Northwest of the Ohio River as early as 1787, and had established the Rectangular Survey System for laying out the land for sale. Well before 1800, several land offices were established in the Ohio River areas to provide close access for settlers wishing to buy land in the newly opened areas.

But the opening of the Old Southwest to public land sales did not begin in earnest until after 1800. The first land sales in the public domain areas of Mississippi Territory were at federal land offices established at the frontier towns of St. Stephens (now in Alabama) and Washington (now in Mississippi). Land sales were limited to areas ceded by the Indians. Because of this, the first land sales in Mississippi Territory were

limited to areas within a radius of 25 miles of Natchez and a small region north of Mobile. The location of the first land sold in Mississippi Territory was not far from water borne access, since there were virtually no overland roads to the area.

The new Rectanglur Survey System was used in the Public Domain of Mississippi Territory. However, since there had been numerous Spanish land grants to private individuals in that area, the United States established a method of honoring these early land grants, proving them in local court proceedings. A holder of a Spanish Land Grant would be required to provide some documentation of his land holdings. The United States then recognized the title to the land and issued another patent to the land holder.

Thus, around the communities of Natchez, Pensacola, Biloxi, and Mobile, the irregular metes and bounds surveys of the colonial land grants can still be observed on land ownership maps. The U.S. established a method of dealing with prior claims of land in Mississippi Territory that was to be followed in most subsequent land acquisitions in Louisiana, Texas, New Mexico, Arizona, and California.

The Federal Horse Path

When Ohio became a state in 1803, the enabling act included a provision that a portion of sales of public lands would be set aside for the purpose of constructing roads in the public lands. Two federally financed roads were to result from this legislation: 1) **The National Road**, from Maryland to Illinois, and 2) **The Federal Road** from Georgia to Louisiana.

Both of these roads were slow to be realized, but by 1830, they had become

America's primary highways. While the barrier to construction of the National Road was the Appalachian Mountains, development of the Federal Road was challenged by the lowland swamps of the Old Southwest. The Federal Road began as a "Horse Path".

In 1805, mail from New Orleans to the new capital at Washington by way of the Natchez Trace took at least two months. The first resident of the newly constructed White House in Washington was not happy with this time delay for communicating with his new territories in the southwestern part of the United States.

In 1806, President Thomas Jefferson signed a law authorizing the construction of a "Horse Path" from the Ocmulgee River of Georgia to New Orleans, Orleans Territory. The road from Augusta, Georgia, to the Creek Indian Agency west of the Ocmulgee River was the southernmost road one could travel by wagon, reached by traveling on either the **Upper Road** or **Fall Line Road** from Virginia, North Carolina, and South Carolina.

The law specified that a riding path was to be built for regular mail service and that

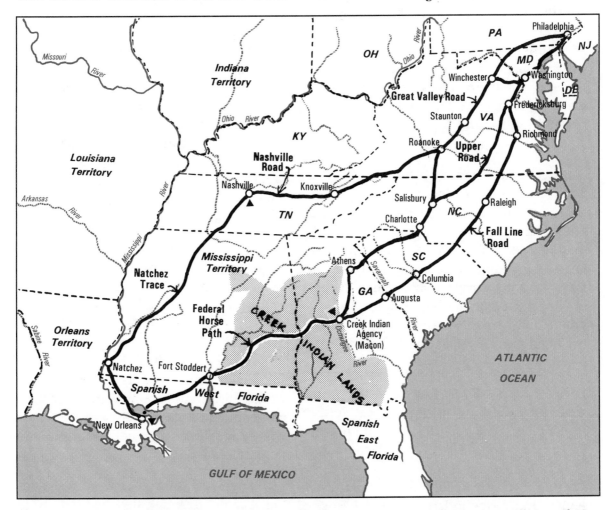

New Orleans to Washington, 1806. Only two overland routes were available for mail out of New Orleans to the new nation's capital in Washington: **The Natchez Trace,** and the **Federal Horse Path.** Much of the Federal Horse Path was within Creek Indian lands. The Federal Government's right to build the Federal Horse Path was provided for in a treaty with the Creek Indians in 1805. After the Louisiana Purchase, the U.S. believed they owned West Florida as well, but Spain disagreed with that opinion. A portion of the Federal Horse Path ran through the disputed West Florida panhandle, an area which was not part of the U.S. until a treaty with Spain in 1812.

the trail and subsequent mail service were to be constructed and operated by the same contractor. The contract required that the road construction should take six months, and thereafter, mail was to be delivered between New Orleans and Washington in no more than 14 days. A year after construction began, mail was still taking about three weeks. The riding trail had several alternative routes the mail carriers discovered were easier to travel than the "improved route".

The Federal Horse Path crossed many lowland areas which required the building of raised causeways through wetlands. In 1806, the entire route from the Ocmulgee River of Georgia to the Mobile River passed through the treaty lands of the Creek Indians. In five years time, this route was to become the **Federal Road,** the most important wagon road of the Old Southwest.

Between the period 1815 to 1840, over 300,000 people used this road to migrate to new settlements in Alabama, Mississippi, Louisiana, Arkansas, and Texas. Most of the migrants left their homes in the Carolinas and Georgia, and came from as far north as Virginia and Maryland. Plantation owners of the Old South moved their entire slave populations, wagons, cattle, equipment, and extended families along the Federal Road to reach richer cotton fields.

The Federal Road was also the prime route for Americans moving to the Mexican province of Texas during the empressario era of the early 1820s. Whole communities of families had the means of travel to Texas via the Federal Road. They would leave homes and farms in large groups. It is said that someone might leave a note on the cabin door, or a local tax collector might write "G.T.T." on the ledger for the missing taxpayer ("Gone To Texas").

The Creek Indians And the War of 1812

In 1805, the United States Government signed a treaty with the Creek Indians which redefined their boundaries and, incidentally, gave the U.S. the right to build and maintain a "horse path" through the Creek lands. The treaty recognized the tribe's autonomy and provided for "passports" to be issued by any of the governors of U.S. states which would allow whites to travel through this "foreign nation". (Many of the passports issued by the governors of Georgia are extant. See Dorothy Williams Potter, *Passports of Southeastern Pioneers,* (Baltimore: Genealogical Publishing Co., Inc., 1982).

The Creeks were asked to operate inns and waystations along the route of the Federal Post Road for the convenience of the riders. Since the road passed almost exclusively through Creek treaty lands, no whites were permitted to settle or engage in business along the route.

But, a war was to change forever this relationship between the Creeks and the U.S. Government. The Creek (or Muscogee) Indians were governed by a loose confederation with several chiefs, some more effective than others. The most prominent of these chiefs was William McIntosh, who sided with the Americans during the War of 1812. Other factions within the Creeks were influenced heavily by the great Tecumseh, who sought a separate nation for all Indians in North America.

In any case, the Creeks were casualties of the War of 1812, defeated by Andrew Jackson's troops. They lost, not only their stature, but their lands, leading to their eventual removal to the Indian Territory in 1838.

The fate of the Creeks was similar to the other "civilized" tribes of the Old Southwest: the Cherokees, Choctaws, Chickasaws, and Seminoles. All of these tribes could be said to be victims of the War of 1812. Having sided with the losing parties of that war, they lost forever to the American whites an area which was at one time nearly one fourth of the total area of the United States.

Land ceded by the five civilized tribes occurred over a period of forty years. By identifying the parcels of land relinquished by treaty with these tribes, the land areas opened to white settlement can be determined. Although there were many cases of

white "squatters" settling on Indian Treaty Lands, they had no legal right to be there until the Indians ceded the land to the U.S. Government.

The Ways South after 1815

In 1811, the United States realized its southern under-belly was vulnerable to British invasion. The U.S. now had new seaports on the Gulf of Mexico in New Orleans, Mobile, Biloxi, and Pensacola. All were exposed to domination by the British Navy should they decide to blockade these ports. For these reasons, the U.S. saw a need for overland access to the Southwest.

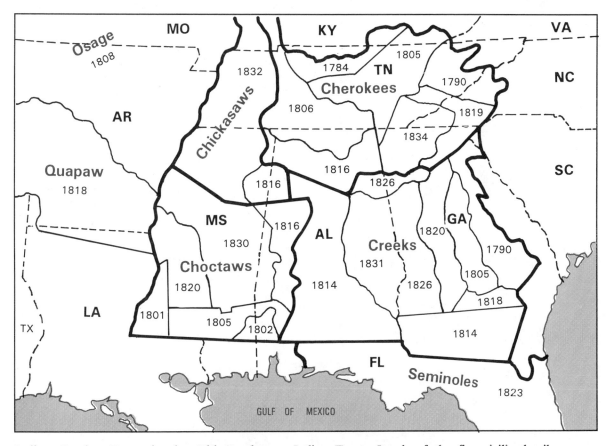

Indian Cession Dates in the Old Southwest. Indian Treaty Lands of the five civilized tribes were systematically reduced in size until 1838 when most of the five tribes were removed to the Indian Territory west of the Mississippi River. The areas shown above reflect the time periods when the various tribes lost control over the lands. Since whites were legally prohibited from settling in these areas, the dates when certain areas were ceded indicates when migrating white families could settle in a particular area of the Old Southwest. The cession dates also indicate the earliest time period for any possible wagon roads into the area.

In 1811, Congress authorized funds to improve existing trails and build new roads in the Old Southwest.

Virtually all of the wagon roads used by migrating families into the Old Southwest were a result of the War of 1812 and the improvement of old Indian trading paths to roads suitable for supporting wagons, cannons, and troops. The roads improved or constructed during the War of 1812 became major migration routes after that war. The wagon roads of the Old Southwest are identified below:

☛ **The Federal Road.** Its eastern approach began at the old Creek Indian Agency on the Ocmulgee River, now Macon, Georgia,

and proceeded through the Creek Indian Lands enroute to New Orleans. The start of the Federal Road became the southern end of the **Fall Line Road,** which approached the Federal Road via Augusta, Georgia. In addition, the **Upper Road** converged on the same point by way of Athens, Georgia. The route to New Orleans followed nearly the same trace as the Federal Horse Path. From Macon, Georgia, this route today is about the same as U.S. Highway 80 via Tuskegee, Alabama, and at Montgomery via what is now Interstate 65 to Mobile, and then Interstate 10 into New Orleans.

☛ **Natchez Trace.** This trail was improved by American troops and after the War of 1812 was commonly known as the **Natchez-**

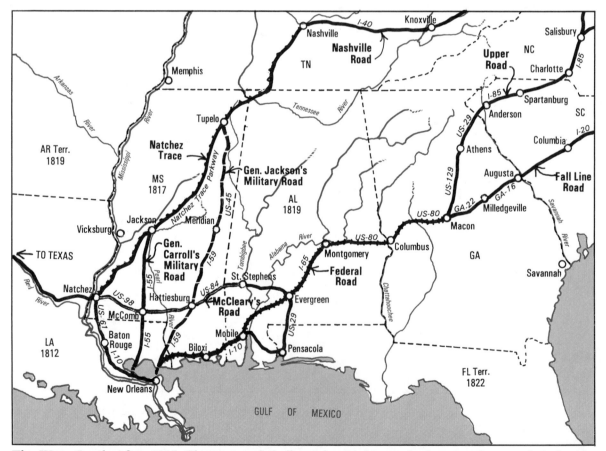

The Ways South After 1815. The new roads built or the existing roads that were improved during the War of 1812 provided the means for moving cannons, wagons, and troops against the British. After the war, these military roads became the primary migration routes to the Old Southwest. The most heavily traveled road was the **Federal Road,** which was the route of some 300,000 people over the twenty-five years following the War of 1812. The Federal Road was also a major route taken by many southern families moving to the Mexican province of Texas in the early 1820s.

Nashville Road. It led from Natchez on the Mississippi River, passing diagonally across the present State of Mississippi, and reaching the Tennessee River near the point where the Alabama, Mississippi, and Tennessee lines come together. The road continued in a northerly direction to Nashville. Today, the Natchez Trace Parkway is a scenic route one can travel nearly full length through Mississippi. Genealogists with ancestors who traveled this route will find the trip worthwhile.

☛ General Jackson's Military Road. During the War of 1812, Andrew Jackson's troops were also responsible for constructing a new road from New Orleans north to the Tombigbee River, providing a more direct route to Nashville, Tennessee. After the war, this road became an important migration route into the Mississippi Valley from Tennessee and Kentucky. Today, the route is nearly the same as Interstate Highway 59 from New Orleans to Meridian, Mississippi. From there, it is about the same as U.S. Highway 45 to Columbus, Mississippi, connecting to the Natchez Trace at Tupelo, Mississippi.

☛ General Carroll's Military Road. This road was constructed by American troops during the War of 1812. It began at New Orleans and proceeded due north to Jackson, Mississippi. The route today is nearly the same as Interstate Highway 55.

☛ McCleary's Road. This trail was improved during the War of 1812 and became an extension of the Federal Road on an east-west line from St. Stephens to Natchez, Mississippi. Today this road is about the same route followed by U.S. Highway 84 to Hattiesburg, and then U.S. Highway 98 to Natchez.

✦ ✦ ✦ ✦ ✦ ✦

Notes

(Refer to page and paragraph beginning with "..........":

Page 1, "However, it was decades....", Albert Bushnell Hart, ed., *American History Told by Contemporaries,* New York: Macmillan Co., 1929, vII, p225.

Page 2, "A German family en route...", P.F.X. de Charlevois, *Journal,* translated by John Gilmary Shea, Ann Arbor: University Microfilms, Inc., 1966, p.221.

Page 4, "But the leg from Fredericksburg...", Benjamin Franklin, *Autobiography,* New York: P.F. Collier & Son, 1962, p.127.

Page 10, "In October 1753....", *Washington's Journal of 1754,* Ann Arbor: University Microfilms, Inc., 1966, v.III, p.115.

Page 13, "Daniel Boone's contribution...", H. Addington Bruce, *Daniel Boone and the Wilderness Road,* New York: Macmillan Co., 1910.

Page 19, (first paragraph) "The boat itself would be....", Robert E. Reigel, *America Moves West,* New York: Holt, Reinhart and Winston, 1930, p.70.

Page 20, In 1796, Ebenezer Zane...", Randall D. Sale and Edwin D. Karn, *American Expansion: A Book of Maps,* Lincoln: Univ. of Nebraska Press, 1979, p.4.

Page 24, "From Canandaigua...", Capt. M. D. Massie, *Past and Present of Pike County, Illinois,* Chicago: S. J. Clarke Publ. Co., 1906, p.680. The story of the Hull family's journey from Canandaigua, New York, to Marietta, Ohio, was in a biographical sketch for a son, John Hull, a resident of Pike County, Illinois.

Page 25, "In the enabling act....", Thomas B. Searight, *The Old Pike: A History of the National Road,* published by the author, 1894. Facsimile reprint, Bowie MD: Heritage Books, Inc., 1990, p. 93.

Other References

Austin, Frederick, *The Old Northwest: A Chronicle of the Ohio Valley and Beyond,* (Chronicles of America Series, vol. 19), New Haven: Yale University Press, 1920.

Billington, Ray A. *Westward Expansion: History of the American Frontier.* New York: Macmillan Co., 1949.

Brannon, Peter A., "The Federal Road - Alabama's First Improved Highway", in *Alabama Highways,* April 1927.

Dunbar, Seymour. *A History of Travel in America.* Indianapolis: Bobbs-Merrill Co., 1915.

Friis, Herman R. *A Series of Population Maps of the Colonies and the United States, 1625-1790,* New York: American Geographical Society, 1968.

Havinghurst, Walter. *Wilderness for Sale.* New York: Hastings House Publishers, 1956.

Holbrook, Steward H. *The Old Post Road.* New York: McGraw-Hill Book Co., 1962.

Hulbert, Archer B., *The Paths of Inland Commerce: A Chronicle of Trail, Road, and Waterway,* (Chronicles of America Series, vol. 21), New Haven: Yale University Press, 1920.

Older, Curtis L., *The Braddock Expedition and Fox's Gap in Maryland,* Westminster, MD: Family Lines Publications, 1995.

Peckham, Howard H. *The Colonial Wars, 1689-1762.* Chicago: University of Chicago Press, 1963.

Paullin, Charles O., *Atlas of the Historical Geography of the United States,* New York: American Geographical Society of New York, 1932.

Riegel, Robert E., and Athearn, R. G. *America Moves West,* 4th ed. New York: Holt, Reinhart and Winston, 1964.

Royce, Charles C., *Indian Cessions in the United States,* (Extract From the Eighteenth Annual Report of the Bureau of American Ethnology), Washington, DC: Government Printing Office, 1900.

Southerland, Henry DeLeon, and Jerry Elijah Brown, *The Federal Road through Georgia, the Creek Nation, and Alabama, 1806-1836,* Tuscaloosa: University of Alabama Press, 1989.

Thorndale, William, and William Dollarhide, *Map Guide to the U.S. Federal Censuses, 1790-1920,* Baltimore: Genealogical Publishing Co., Inc., 1987.

Waitley, Douglas. *Roads of Destiny: the Trails that Shaped a Nation.* New York: Robert B. Luce, Inc., 1970.

✦ ✦ ✦ ✦ ✦

Index

Heritage Quest
M a g a z i n e

Dear Genealogy Enthusiast:

HERITAGE QUEST would like to make you a sensational offer! We'll give you a FREE copy of America's leading genealogy magazine. We're confident that once you review one of our issues you'll be hooked.

No matter what your genealogy experience--beginning, intermediate or advanced--our authors engage you at each level. You'll be able to glean expertise from acclaimed genealogists such as Horst Reschke; syndicated columnist, Myra Vanderpool Gormely; and Internet guru, Cyndi Howells.

Risk nothing! Act now to receive your complimentary review copy. It's yours to keep--regardless. If you like the magazine, pay just $24.95 for the year (that's six full issues for $16.75 off cover price). Does it get any better? Don't just take my word for it, respond now and see for yourself!

Regards,

Steve Williams
Steve Williams
VP Sales & Marketing

P.S. Subscription rates have never been lower, so act now to lock-in the special subscription price. Return the attached postcard or phone: 1-800-658-7755.

Let the genealogy experts help you. *Heritage Quest*—America's premiere genealogy magazine—is packed with over 20 articles by seasoned experts. Each issue of *Heritage Quest* informs genealogists and family historians with 144 pages of how-to, resources, tips and techniques focused on your needs. No other genealogical magazine provides that much content.

www.heritagequest.com

Here's what the experts are saying:
"*Heritage Quest* is one of my 'must read' magazines, I go through it cover ● cover as soon as it arrives."
Dick Eastman, Eastman's Online Genealogy Newsletter

...An excellent reference tool for not only the beginning genealogist but also for the advanced researcher.
Karen Clifford, AG
If genealogy is your hobby or your vocation, you need this magazine!

Tear along dotted line, place stamp as indicated, and mail bottom half.

ame _____

ddress _____

ty _____ state _____ zip _____

√ **YES,** I'd like to sample a FREE issue of *Heritage Quest Magazine.* If I like my FREE sample issue, I'll receive 6 more issues for $24.95. I'll save $16.75 off the newsstand price—that's over **40% off** the annual cover price.

If I choose not to subscribe, I'll return your subscription bill marked "cancel" and owe nothing.

The FREE issue of *Heritage Quest Magazine* will be mine to keep—with no hassle, no obligation, and no questions asked.

PLEASE
PLACE
STAMP
HERE

Heritage Quest
M a g a z i n e

Subscription Department
PO Box 329
Bountiful, UT 84011-0329